RUTH HEPHZIBAH

VOLUME 1

A Pen That
REWRITES GRIEF

A 60-DAY DEVOTIONAL AND HEALING JOURNAL

HEY, I'M RUTH

I am a Qualified Mental Health Specialist, a Psychosocial rehabilitation Specialist, and a qualified skills Specialist. I specialize in providing Grief transition coaching at Grief to Grace (G2G) for people working through life's most challenging seasons. People call me when they want to get "unstuck," and I educate them through the "mud.

Three years ago, I lost my husband, Mother-in-law, father-in-law, and 2 friends in a span of a year. I lost myself; I lost my identity, self-esteem, and willpower. I was stuck and never thought I could ever rise again. I lost everything. The strategies shared here are tools that have helped me and so many people in my network.

Ruth Hephzibah

LET'S DO IT!

Welcome

Welcome to "A Pen That Rewrites Grief," a haven for those navigating the often-challenging path of loss. Whether you've recently experienced a loss or are carrying the weight of one from the past, know this: you are not alone.

This 60-day devotional and journal is offered as a gentle companion on your journey. We will explore the complexities of grief, cultivate self-compassion, and discover the strength to move forward with renewed hope.

Imagine yourself standing at a crossroads. One path leads back into the darkness of sorrow; the other leads toward a future filled with light and possibility. While the journey ahead may be uncertain, the strength to navigate it lies within you.

Over the next Sixty days, we will explore themes of:
- Understanding and navigating grief
- Finding compassion for yourself and others
- Uncovering meaning and purpose amidst loss
- Practicing self-care and nurturing your well-being
- Embracing hope and the possibility of joy
-

Each day in "A Pen That Rewrites Grief" offers:

- A short reflection to guide your thoughts and emotions.
- A comforting message or prayer for solace and strength.
- An actionable step to encourage healing and growth.
- Ample journaling space to capture your reflections, feelings, and personal journey.
-

Remember, this is your journey. Take what resonates with you and leave the rest behind. Allow yourself to feel deeply, question freely, and move at your own pace.

Together, with the help of this book, you can begin to rewrite your narrative of grief, one compassionate step and heartfelt entry at a time.

Ruth Hephzibah

Let's Rewrite This Story

Hey There,

Grief, right? It feels like a ton of bricks just landed on your life, shutting out the sun. Maybe you just went through a loss, or perhaps the echo still hangs around. Whatever it is, you're not alone in this.

This book, "A Pen That Rewrites Grief," is here to be your buddy on this journey. It's a 60-day devotional and journal but think of it as a pep talk in your pocket.

Imagine you're standing at a crossroads. Behind you is this whole landscape of loss, filled with memories and maybe some tears. But in front of you? That's an entire horizon, a blank canvas waiting for your story.

Over the next Sixtyty days, we're going to explore some stuff that'll help you navigate this new path:

Understanding your grief: We'll break down what's going on in your head and heart so you can deal with it head-on.

Self-compassion? More like self-care, boss! We'll learn how to be kind to ourselves because, trust me, you deserve it.

Finding meaning in loss: Even though it hurts, there can be a purpose. We'll help you discover that purpose.

Taking care of yourself: We'll explore ways to nourish your mind, body, and spirit so you can be vital for whatever comes next.

Embracing hope, even when it's scary: Grief might stick around, but so can happiness and the excitement of what's to come.

Each day in "A Pen That Rewrites Grief" will give you:

- A reflection to get you thinking about your stuff.
- A message or prayer to keep you feeling supported.
- An action step to move you forward, one step at a time.

The journal has plenty of space to write down your thoughts, feelings, and whatever else pops into your head.

This is your journey, your story to rewrite. Take what works for you; leave what doesn't. Use the journal to vent, ask questions, and track your progress.

With this pen, you can rewrite your story. Each stroke will transform grief from a burden into a stepping stone. You'll build resilience, find hope, and embrace a new chapter filled with possibility.

So, are you ready to rewrite this story? Let's do this.

Your Journey

Before We Begin...

As we embark on the journey with "A Pen That Rewrites Grief," I want to pause and ask: What do you hope to achieve with the transformative power of this book? What emotions do you wish to explore, understand, and ultimately transform through the act of writing?

Your intentions hold the key to unlocking this journey's healing potential. Whether you seek solace, catharsis, or a deeper understanding of your grief, your aspirations are central to our co-create narrative.

Take a moment to reflect on your intentions for engaging with "A Pen That Rewrites Grief," and know that your journey begins with the power of your pen. Remember, only you can rewrite your story.

With empathy and encouragement,

Ruth Hephzibah

JUST KEEP
MOVING
FORWARD
Ruth Hephzibah

01 Introduction to the Journey

Welcome to the beginning of your journey from grief to grace. Take a moment to reflect on these two powerful concepts: grief and grace.

Grief is a natural response to loss, a complex emotion that can weigh heavy on the heart. It manifests in many forms: sadness, anger, and confusion. It's okay to feel these emotions deeply.

Grace, on the other hand, is the gentle hand that guides us through the storms of life. The light shines through the cracks, offering hope and solace. Grace is the strength to carry on, even when the burden feels overwhelming.

As you embark on this journey, know it won't be easy. There will be days when grief threatens to consume you when the pain feels unbearable. But there will also be moments of grace – small, quiet moments that remind you of the beauty and resilience of the human spirit.

Embrace both grief and grace with an open heart. Allow yourself to feel deeply, to mourn the losses you've experienced. And hold onto grace tightly, for it will carry you through the darkest times.

Take this first step with courage and faith. You are not alone on this journey. Together, we will walk from grief to grace.

Reflection: What does grief mean to you? How do you envision grace guiding you through this journey?

Action: Take a few moments to journal your thoughts and feelings about grief and grace. Allow yourself to be honest and vulnerable.

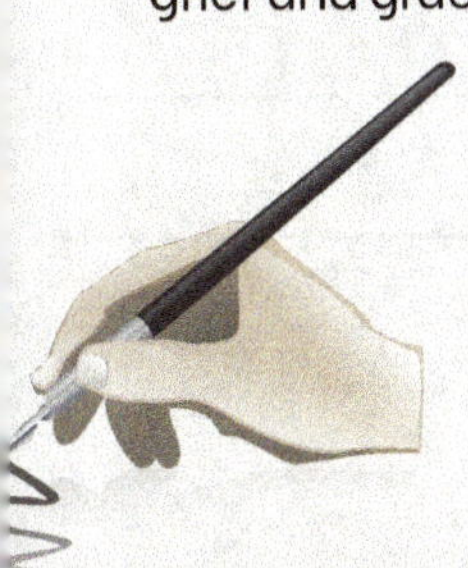

YOUR NOTES:

Enjoy the process

02 Acknowledge Your Grief

Grief is a natural response to loss, a journey of emotions that can be both overwhelming and transformative. Today, take a moment to acknowledge your grief. Allow yourself to sit with your feelings, to experience them fully without judgment or resistance. Whether your grief is fresh or old, raw or muted, it deserves to be seen and heard.

Reflection: How does your grief feel? How does it manifest in your body, mind, and spirit?

Action: Find a quiet space to be alone with your thoughts and feelings. Take several deep breaths, allowing yourself to connect with the sensations of grief. Write down whatever comes to mind – memories, regrets, hopes. Allow yourself to release whatever needs to be expressed.

YOUR NOTES:

Enjoy the process

03 The Inkwell of Tears

The title, "The Inkwell of Tears," paints a vivid image. Imagine a well overflowing with dark, inky liquid, representing the overwhelming emotions of grief. Loss feels like a hurricane that rips through our lives, leaving a trail of devastation. Tears are a natural response, a way for our bodies to release physical and emotional pain. Don't feel pressured to erase these tears right away. They are a necessary part of the healing process. Just like fertile soil needs rain to nurture new life, grief needs tears to begin healing.

Reflection:
What emotions come up for you when you think about your grief? Sadness? Anger? Loneliness?
Where in your body do you feel the pain? Does it tighten your chest or make your throat ache?

Action:
Find a quiet space where you can cry freely. If journaling helps, write down your feelings without judgment. Alternatively, express yourself creatively through music, art, or poetry. Let the tears flow like cleansing rain.

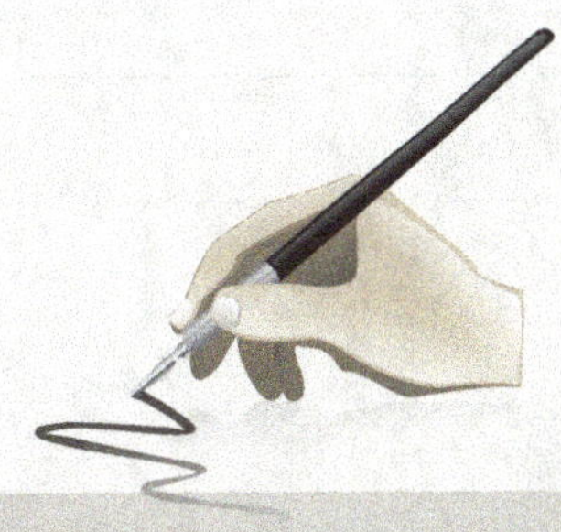

YOUR NOTES:

Enjoy the process

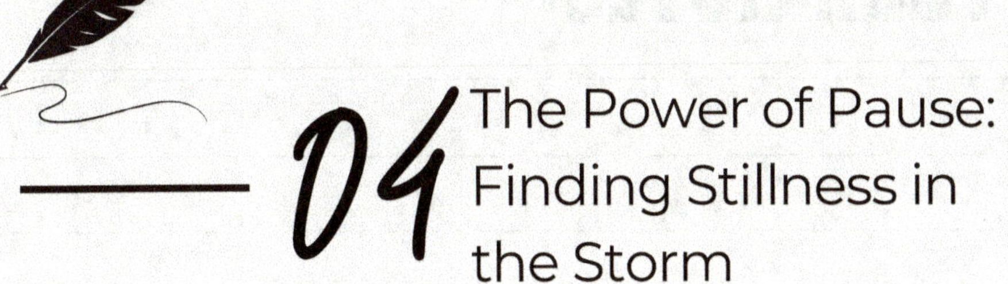

04 The Power of Pause: Finding Stillness in the Storm

Grief is not a linear journey. There will be days when the urge to rewrite is strong and others where you need to pause. Today, the title "The Power of Pause" reminds us of the importance of allowing ourselves space to breathe. Sit with the silence, breathe deeply, and listen to the whispers of your heart. Let the storm of emotions subside, even for a moment.

Reflection:
What does your body need right now? Rest? Movement? Connection? How can you honor those needs with kindness and compassion?

Action:
Practice mindfulness exercises like meditation or deep breathing. Spend time in nature, allowing the peace of the outdoors to soothe your spirit. Listen to calming music or curl up with a comforting book. Permit yourself to be.

YOUR NOTES:

Enjoy the process

05 Finding Comfort

Amid grief's storm, comfort can be found in unexpected places. Today, open your heart to receive comfort. It may come in the form of a warm embrace from a loved one, the soothing melody of a favorite song, or the gentle whisper of nature. Allow yourself to be held by these moments of solace, knowing that you are not alone.

Reflection: What brings you comfort during times of grief? How can you cultivate more comfort in your life?

Action: Create a comfort corner in your home – a cozy space filled with items that bring you joy and peace. Spend a few moments there each day to rest and recharge.

YOUR NOTES:

Enjoy the process

06 Embracing Grace

Grace is the gentle hand that guides us through the darkest of nights. Today, open yourself to the possibility of grace. Notice the small miracles surrounding you – the kindness of a stranger, the beauty of a sunrise, the resilience of the human spirit. Embrace these moments of grace with gratitude and humility, knowing they are gifts to be cherished.

Reflection: How have you experienced grace in your life? What does it feel like to be held by grace?

Action: Practice acts of grace today – extend kindness to yourself and others, forgive past hurts, and embrace each moment with an open heart.

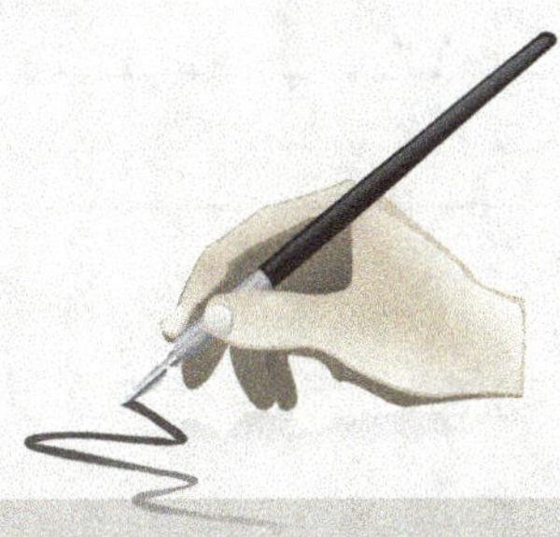

YOUR NOTES:

____

____

____

____

____

____

____

____

____

____

____

____

____

____

____

Enjoy the process

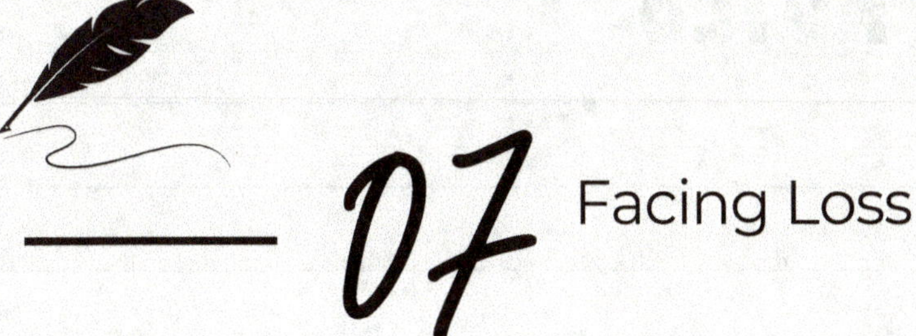

07 Facing Loss

Loss is an inevitable part of the human experience, a thread woven into the fabric of life. Today, honor the losses you've experienced. Whether it's the death of a loved one, the end of a relationship, or the loss of a dream, each loss leaves its mark on our hearts. Allow yourself to grieve fully, knowing that healing begins through mourning.

Reflection: What losses have you faced in your life? How have they shaped you as a person?

Action: Create a memorial to honor your losses – light a candle, plant a tree, or create a piece of art representing your dear memories. Spend time reflecting on the impact of these losses on your life journey.

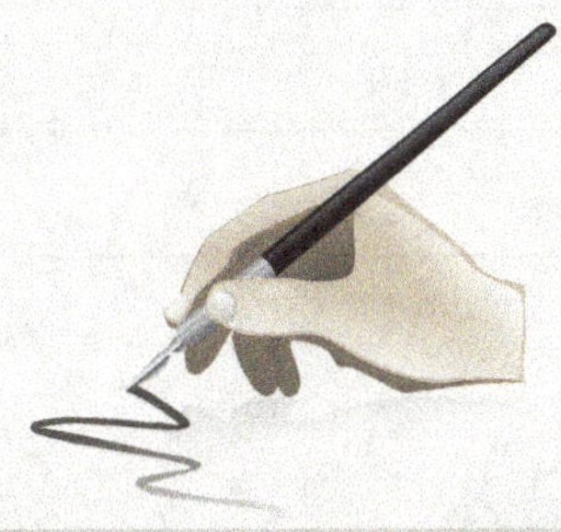

YOUR NOTES:

Enjoy the process

08 Hope in the Darkness

In the depths of grief, hope can seem like a distant star in a blackened sky. Yet, it is in these moments of darkness that hope shines brightest. Today, allow yourself to embrace the hope that flickers within you. Remember that even the longest night must eventually give way to dawn. Hold onto hope with unwavering faith, knowing it will guide you through the darkest times.

Reflection: Where do you find hope in times of darkness? How does hope sustain you on your journey?

Action: Create a hope jar by writing down hopeful thoughts, quotes, or affirmations on small pieces of paper. Whenever you feel overwhelmed by grief, reach into the jar and read a message of hope to lift your spirits.

YOUR NOTES:

Enjoy the process

09 Practicing Self-Compassion

When grieving, it's easy to be hard on yourself – to criticize, judge, and condemn. Today, practice the art of self-compassion. Treat yourself with the kindness and understanding you would offer a dear friend. Embrace your imperfections with love and acceptance, knowing you are worthy of compassion, especially in times of sorrow.

Reflection: How do you talk to yourself during moments of grief? Are your words filled with kindness or criticism?

Action: Write yourself a love letter expressing compassion and understanding for all you are going through. Read it aloud, allowing the words to sink deep into your soul.

YOUR NOTES:

Enjoy the process

Finding Strength in Community: You Are Not Alone

Grief can feel isolating, but the title "Finding Strength in Community" reminds us that we are not alone. Contact friends, family, or support groups who understand what you're going through. Sharing your pain with others can be a powerful source of strength and comfort. Imagine a circle of loved ones holding you up, their love a steady force against the waves of grief.

Reflection:
Who in your life offers a listening ear and supportive presence? How can you connect with others who have experienced Loss?

Action:
You can connect with a grief counselor, attend a support group meeting, or contact a trusted friend or family member for a conversation. You can also consider joining an online community dedicated to grief support.

YOUR NOTES:

Enjoy the process

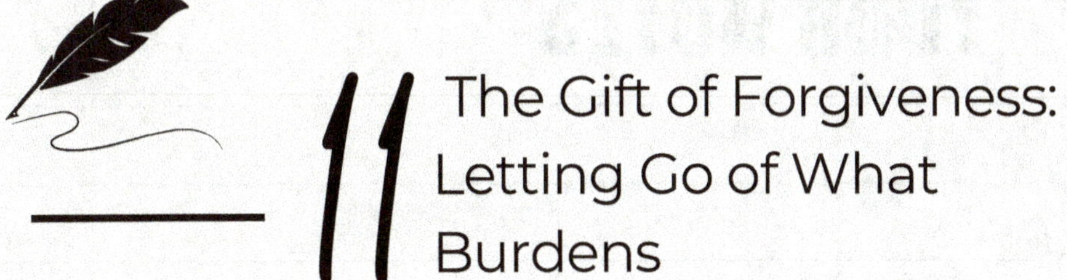

11 The Gift of Forgiveness: Letting Go of What Burdens

Grief often comes hand-in-hand with anger, resentment, or even guilt. These emotions, like heavy weights, can hinder the rewriting process. The title "The Gift of Forgiveness" signifies the power of releasing negativity. Forgiveness is not condoning actions but setting yourself free from the burden of those emotions. Imagine a bird, finally released from a cage, soaring towards the light.

Reflection:
Are there any unresolved issues or words left unsaid with the person you lost?
Can you find the courage to forgive yourself or them (if applicable)?

Action:
Write a forgiveness letter, even if it's never sent. Consider practicing self-compassion exercises to release any guilt you may be holding onto. Remember, forgiveness is a gift you give yourself, allowing you to move forward.

YOUR NOTES:

Enjoy the process

12 The Gentle Touch of Gratitude: Finding Light in the Darkness

The title, "The Gentle Touch of Gratitude," acknowledges the unexpected beauty that can emerge from grief. While Loss casts a long shadow, there's still room for appreciation. Think of a single flower blooming through a crack in the pavement. Be grateful for the memories you shared, the love that enriched your life, and the strength you possess to navigate this difficult path.

Reflection:

What are you grateful for in your life, even amidst the grief?
Is it the support of loved ones, the beauty of nature, or a newfound appreciation for simple things?

Action:

Start a gratitude journal. Write down three things you're thankful for each day, no matter how small.

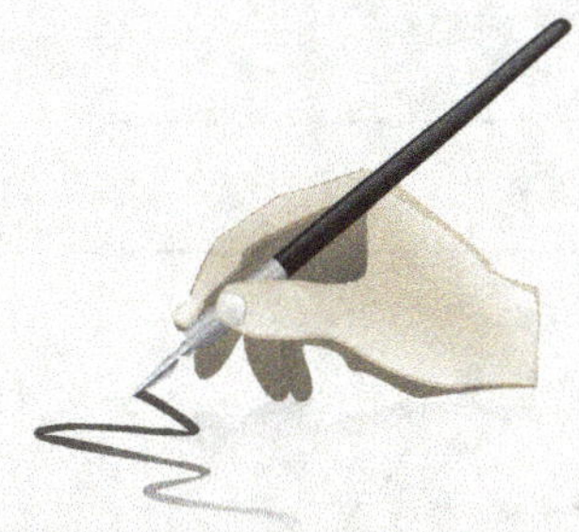

YOUR NOTES:

Enjoy the process

13 The Colors of Healing: Embracing the Journey

Grief is not a monochrome experience. The title, "The Colors of Healing," reminds us that there will be moments of joy, laughter, and even peace alongside the sadness. Imagine a painting, initially dominated by dark hues, slowly incorporating brighter colors as healing progresses. Embrace the full spectrum of emotions as you move forward.

Reflection:
What activities bring you joy or peace, even for a short time? How can you incorporate these activities into your healing journey?

Action:
Engage in hobbies you enjoy, spend time with loved ones who make you laugh, or explore activities that calm you.

YOUR NOTES:

Enjoy the process

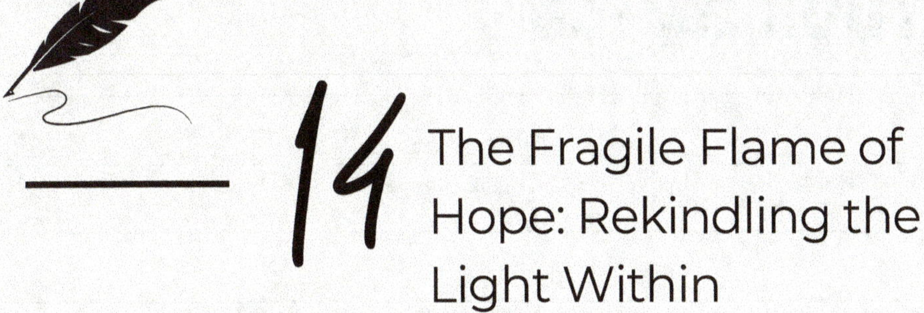

14 The Fragile Flame of Hope: Rekindling the Light Within

Grief can extinguish our inner flame, leaving us feeling lost in darkness. The title, "The Fragile Flame of Hope," signifies the importance of reigniting that spark. Imagine a flickering candle, its light barely visible. Like a gentle breeze, hope can nurture that flame back to life. Look for minor signs of hope, a kind word from a friend, a beautiful sunset, or a personal achievement.

Reflection:
What are some things you used to look forward to in life?
How can you reconnect with those interests or passions, even in a modified form?

Action:
Set small, achievable goals for yourself. It could be taking a walk in nature, reading a book chapter, or spending time on a creative project. Celebrate each accomplishment, no matter how small.

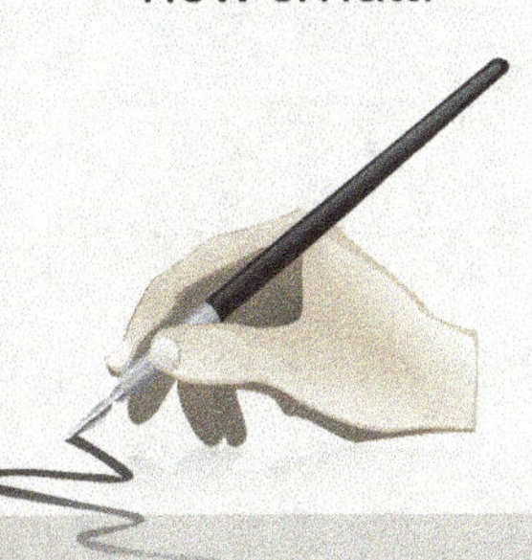

YOUR NOTES:

Enjoy the process

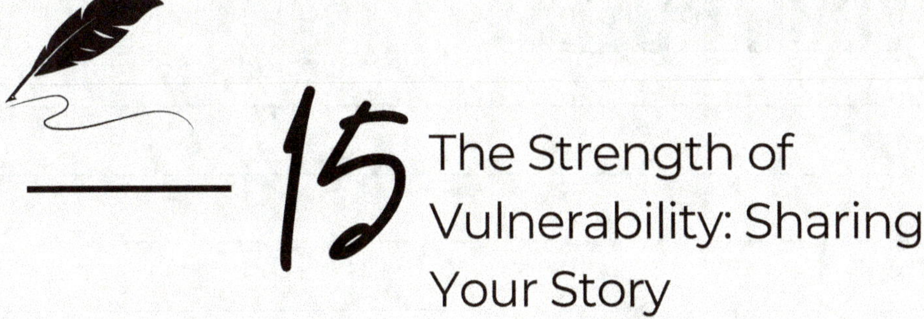

15 The Strength of Vulnerability: Sharing Your Story

Sharing your grief with others can be a daunting prospect. Yet, the title, "The Strength of Vulnerability," underscores the power of connection. Imagine a bridge connecting you to others who understand your pain. Sharing your story can be incredibly cathartic and foster a sense of belonging.

Reflection:
Is there someone you trust with whom you can openly share your grief?
Would you consider joining a grief support group or online forum?

Action:
Contact a trusted friend, family member, therapist, or grief counselor. Sharing your story can be a decisive step towards healing.

YOUR NOTES:

Enjoy the process

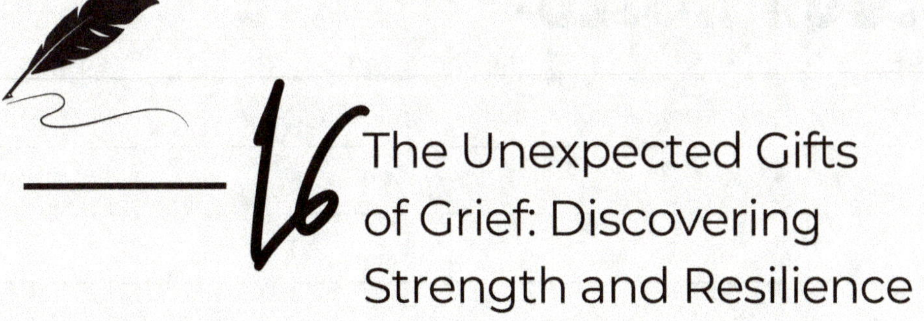

The Unexpected Gifts of Grief: Discovering Strength and Resilience

Grief can reveal hidden depths of strength and resilience within us. The title, "The Unexpected Gifts of Grief," acknowledges the unexpected ways Loss can shape us. Imagine a flower pushing through hard rock, its delicate beauty belying its tenacity. Grief can make us more compassionate, empathetic, and appreciative of life's precious moments.

Reflection:

In what ways has your experience with grief made you stronger or more resilient?
How can you use those newfound qualities to navigate life's challenges?

Action:

Consider volunteering your time or supporting a cause close to your heart. Helping others can be a powerful way to find meaning and purpose.

YOUR NOTES:

Enjoy the process

17 Finding Meaning

Grief is a way of stripping away the superficial layers of life and leaving behind the raw essence of our existence. Today, seek meaning during grief. Reflect on the lessons you have learned, the wisdom you have gained, and the person you are becoming due to your experiences. Find purpose in your pain, knowing that even the darkest moments can lead to profound transformation.

Reflection: What meaning can you find in your experiences of grief? How have they shaped your journey?

Action: Plant and nurture a seedling as a symbol of new growth and renewal. As the plant thrives, reflect on how you are growing and evolving from grief to grace.

YOUR NOTES:

18 Healing Through Creativity

Creativity has the power to heal wounds of the heart and soul. Today, embrace the healing power of creativity to navigate grief. Engage in a creative activity that speaks to your soul—painting, writing, gardening, or dancing. Allow yourself to express your emotions freely, letting creativity guide the journey toward healing.

Reflection: How does creativity help you process grief? What creative activities bring you solace and joy?

Action: Set aside time today to engage in a creative activity that nourishes your soul. Let go of any expectations or judgments and allow yourself to be fully immersed in the creative process.

YOUR NOTES:

Enjoy the process

19 The Power of Community

Grief can feel isolating and lonely but remember you are not alone on this journey. Today, reflect on the power of community in times of sorrow—contact friends, family, or support groups who can offer empathy, understanding, and companionship. Allow yourself to lean on others for support and share your burdens with those who care about you.

Reflection: Who are the members of your support network? List them and reach out to them. How can you lean on them for strength and solace?

Action: Reach out to someone in your community experiencing grief and offer them a listening ear or a comforting word. By supporting others, you also nurture your healing journey.

YOUR NOTES:

Enjoy the process

20 Forgiveness

Forgiveness is the bedrock of freedom from the shackles of grief. It is a powerful tool for healing and liberation. Today, explore the role of forgiveness in your journey from grief to grace. Reflect on any resentments, grudges, or hurts that you are holding onto, and consider the possibility of letting them go. Forgiveness does not condone the actions of others. Still, it frees you from carrying anger and bitterness in your heart. Remember, in this journey, you must forgive yourself, the person involved, and the event associated with the grieving moments. Forgiveness is a crucial component if you desire healing. Nothing is worth the stress.

Reflection: Whom must you forgive to move forward on your healing journey? What would it look like to release resentment and embrace forgiveness?

Action: Write a letter of forgiveness—whether to yourself, someone who has hurt you, or to a higher power. Pour your heart into the letter, expressing your willingness to relinquish past grievances and embrace peace.

YOUR NOTES:

Enjoy the process

21 Embracing Change

Change is an inevitable part of life, especially after grief. Today, embrace the changes due to your experiences with loss. While change can be difficult and painful, it also holds the potential for growth and renewal. Embrace change as an opportunity to cultivate resilience and adaptability on your journey from grief to grace.

Reflection: How have you changed as a result of your experiences with grief? What aspects of change do you find most challenging or rewarding?

Action: Take a walk in nature and observe the changes happening around you – the shifting seasons, the budding flowers, the flowing river. Allow these natural changes to remind you of the beauty and impermanence of life, and find peace in the knowledge that change is a natural part of the human experience.

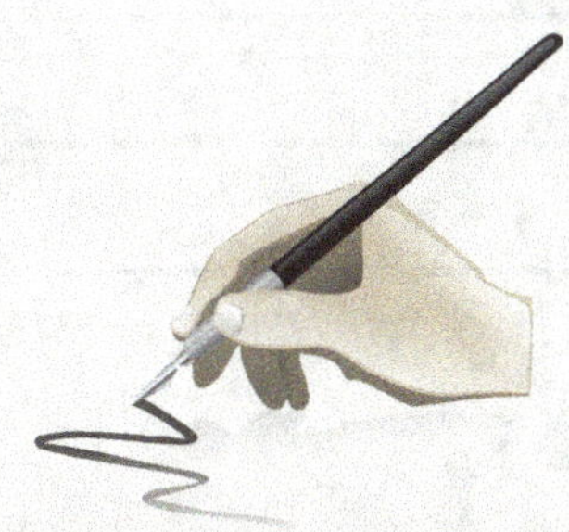

YOUR NOTES:

Enjoy the process

22 Finding Joy

Joy may feel elusive in the midst of grief, but it still exists, waiting to be rediscovered. Today, seek out moments of joy and gratitude amidst the pain. Notice the small blessings in your life—a gentle breeze, a warm embrace, a shared laugh. Embrace these moments with open arms, allowing joy to permeate your heart and lift your spirits.

Reflection: What brings you joy in moments of sorrow? How can you cultivate more happiness in your life?

Action: Create a joy jar by writing down moments of joy and gratitude on slips of paper. Whenever you're feeling down, reach into the jar and read a reminder of the beauty and goodness in your life.

YOUR NOTES:

Enjoy the process

23 Letting Go

Grief can be accompanied by a sense of clinging to what was, but true healing often requires letting go. Today, practice the art of letting go – releasing attachments to the past, expectations for the future, and judgments about the present. Trust that letting go creates space for new beginnings and fresh possibilities to emerge.

Reflection: What are you holding onto that no longer serves you? What would it look like to release it?

Action: Take a symbolic action of letting go – release a helium balloon into the sky, write down what you're letting go of on a piece of paper and burn it, or visualize releasing your attachments and surrendering to the flow of life.

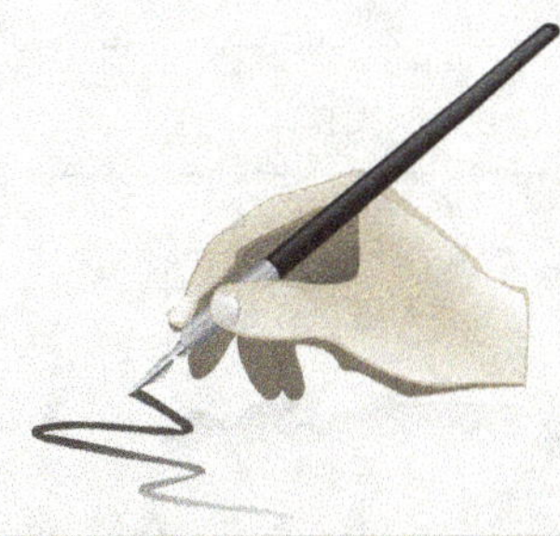

YOUR NOTES:

Enjoy the process

24 Unburdening Your Heart: Letting Go of Resentment's Chains

Grief can be a heavy cloak woven with threads of sorrow, anger, and even resentment. Perhaps there are unresolved words with the one you lost or a lingering sense of what could have been. It's natural to feel these things, but holding onto them is like wearing heavy chains. They weigh you down, making it hard to move forward.

Imagine yourself standing in a beautiful meadow, bound by these heavy chains. Forgiveness isn't about condoning actions or erasing the pain. It's about choosing to unlock those chains, step into the sunlight, and feel the weight lift from your heart. It's a gift you give yourself, a chance to find peace amidst the storm.

Reflection:

Close your eyes and take a deep breath. What emotions come up for you when you think about the one you lost? Is there anger, hurt, or maybe even guilt? It's okay to feel these things. Please spend a few moments acknowledging them without judgment.

Action:

Today, we'll take a small step toward letting go. Find a quiet space and write a letter to the person you lost. Express your honest feelings, both sadness and anger. You don't have to send it, but allow yourself to release these emotions on paper. Imagine the chains loosening with each word you write, and feel a gentle light bloom within your heart.

YOUR NOTES:

Enjoy the process

25 The Healing Power of Self-Compassion: Forgiving Yourself

Sometimes, grief can sound like a harsh inner critic whispering doubts and regrets. Maybe you said something you wish you could take back or feel you didn't do enough. My dear friend, please remember that we are all human and make mistakes. The one you loved wouldn't want you to carry this burden.

Imagine holding a small, wounded bird in your hand. You wouldn't scold it for being hurt; instead, you would offer it gentle care and love. Extend the same compassion to yourself. Forgive yourself for any perceived shortcomings. You did your best with the knowledge you had at the time.

Reflection:

Take a moment to reflect. Are you holding onto guilt or regret related to your Loss? Perhaps you need to take advantage of opportunities for shared moments or words left unspoken. Now, imagine holding yourself with kindness. What words of comfort and understanding would you offer a loved one in the same situation?

Action:

Today, let's practice self-compassion. Write down a list of things you appreciate about yourself, your strengths, and your unique qualities. Remind yourself that you are worthy of love and forgiveness, especially from yourself.

YOUR NOTES:

Enjoy the process

26 Forgiveness: A Journey, Not a Destination

The path of forgiveness can feel long and winding. There will be days when it feels like a heavyweight, and that's perfectly okay. Forgiveness is a journey, not a destination. Imagine yourself slowly climbing a mountain, each step a conscious choice to let go. With every act of self-compassion or positive memory, the weight lessens, and the view from the top becomes clearer.

Be patient with yourself. Some days, forgiveness might feel like an impossible mountain to climb. But remember, you are not alone on this journey. Take a deep breath, and allow yourself to feel whatever emotions arise. It's okay to cry, to be angry, and to miss the one you loved dearly.

Reflection:

How does the concept of forgiveness make you feel? Is it daunting, liberating, or somewhere in between? Take a moment to acknowledge these emotions without judgment. There's no right or wrong way to feel, and the path to forgiveness will unfold at its own pace.

Action:

Today, choose a calming activity that brings you peace. It could be meditation, deep breathing exercises, or simply spending time in nature. Allow yourself to be present in the moment, and trust that forgiveness will blossom in its own time. Remember, you are strong, you are loved, and you are worthy of healing.

YOUR NOTES:

Enjoy the process

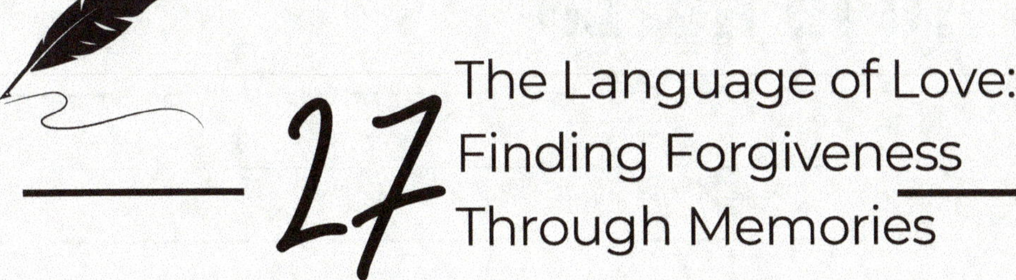

27 The Language of Love: Finding Forgiveness Through Memories

Grief can distort memories, painting them with the harsh colors of anger and blame. Today, let's explore a different path. Imagine opening a dusty photo album filled with cherished moments shared with the one you lost. Each picture is a testament to the love that existed, a reminder of your shared laughter and joy.

Focus on a memory that brings a smile to your face. Recall their kindness and humor and how they made you feel loved and accepted. Let the warmth of that memory wash over you, softening the edges of resentment. Forgiveness doesn't erase the pain but allows those beautiful memories to coexist with your sadness.

Reflection:

Close your eyes and take a few deep breaths. Can you recall a specific memory of the one you lost that fills you with love and warmth? A shared inside joke, a particular tradition, or a simple act of kindness. Hold onto that memory, allowing it to bring a sense of peace amidst the grief.

Action:

Create a memory box or digital album filled with photos, handwritten notes, or even small trinkets with special meaning. As you gather these mementos, allow yourself to reminisce about the love and joy they brought into your life. Remember, forgiveness doesn't erase the pain but will enable the love to shine through.

YOUR NOTES:

Enjoy the process

28 Forgiveness as Freedom: Releasing Yourself from the Past

Imagine yourself standing at a crossroads. One path leads back into the darkness of anger and resentment; the other leads forward into the light of hope and healing. Forgiveness is choosing the path forward, a conscious act of setting yourself free from the prison of the past. Holding onto anger and blame is like carrying a heavy stone in your backpack. It weighs you down and hinders your ability to move forward. Forgiveness allows you to gently place that stone down, lighten your load, and walk with newfound freedom. You are not condoning actions but choosing peace for yourself.

Reflection:

Imagine you could have a conversation with the person you lost one last time. What would you say? Would you express anger and blame or speak from a place of love and understanding? Take a moment to ponder this question, and allow your heart to guide you.

Action:

Today, practice a loving-kindness meditation. Visualize yourself surrounded by a warm, golden light. Extend that light outwards, first to yourself, then to the person you lost, and finally to everyone in your life. As you do this, repeat a mantra of love and forgiveness, such as "May I be filled with peace" or "May I be free from suffering." Remember, forgiveness is a gift you give yourself, a chance to find peace and move forward with an open heart.

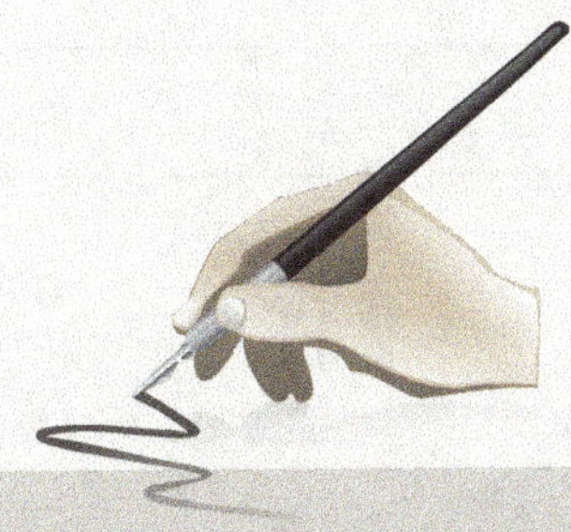

YOUR NOTES:

Enjoy the process

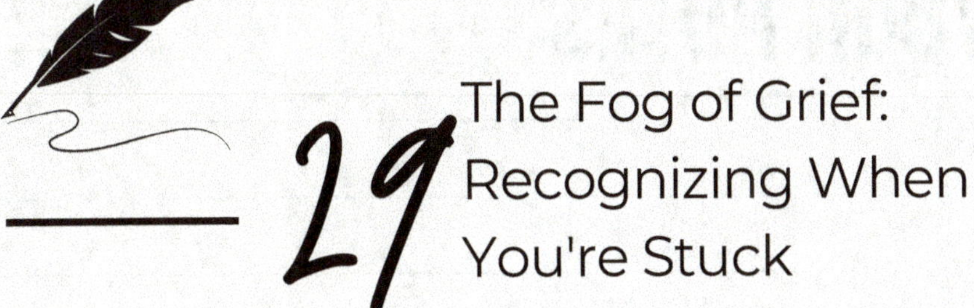

29 The Fog of Grief: Recognizing When You're Stuck

Grief is a journey, not a destination. There will be days when the path feels clear and others when you find yourself lost in a thick fog. This fog represents those moments when you feel stuck, unable to move forward. It's normal to experience periods of intense sadness, anger, or even a sense of numbness.

But how do you know when you're genuinely stuck? The fog has become constant, making it difficult to function daily. You may be avoiding social interactions, neglecting responsibilities, or clinging to the past in a way that hinders the present.

Reflection:

Take a moment to reflect on your current state. Are there specific emotions that dominate your daily life? Has grief significantly impacted your ability to function or cope? Notice these signs without judgment. Recognizing you're stuck is the first step toward finding your way out of the fog.

Action:

Today, commit to a small act of self-care. It could be a relaxing bath, a walk in nature, or simply enjoying a cup of tea in your favorite spot. Taking care of yourself, even in small ways, can help you see through the fog and rediscover your inner strength.

YOUR NOTES:

Enjoy the process

30   A Beacon in the Fog: Seeking Support and Guidance

Navigating the fog of grief can be overwhelming. Imagine yourself adrift at sea, lost and unsure of the way forward. But fear not; there's a beacon in the distance, a symbol of hope and guidance. This beacon represents the support system that surrounds you – friends, family, therapists, or even grief support groups.

Reaching out for help is not a sign of weakness; it's a sign of strength. Talking to others who understand your pain can provide a sense of validation and connection. A therapist can offer tools and strategies to manage emotions and develop healthy coping mechanisms.

Reflection:

Think about the people in your life who offer love and support. Is there someone you trust enough to confide in about your struggles? Consider exploring grief support groups or online forums to connect with others who share your experience.

Action:

Today, take a step towards building a support network. Reach out to a friend or family member who has been there for you. Contact a local grief counselor or explore online support groups for loss patients. Remember, you don't have to navigate this journey alone.

YOUR NOTES:

Enjoy the process

31 The Unanswerable Question: Accepting the Mystery

Grief often comes with a relentless question: "Why?" Why did this happen? Why them? Why now? It's natural to seek answers, to understand the cosmic plan that feels so cruel. But sometimes, the truth is, there may be a vague answer.

Imagine yourself standing at the edge of a vast ocean. Powerful and unpredictable waves crash against the shore. Loss can feel like that—a force beyond our control that leaves us questioning the meaning behind the storm.

Reflection:

Take a moment to acknowledge the "Why" question within you. Let it exist without judgment. Now, imagine a calm space within yourself, a place of acceptance. Can you allow the question to coexist with this newfound peace, even if the answer remains elusive?

Action:

Today, practice mindfulness meditation. Focus on your breath, feeling the rise and fall of your chest. Allow intrusive thoughts, including the "Why," to come and go without attaching to them. Acceptance doesn't erase the pain but allows you to find peace amidst the mystery.

YOUR NOTES:

Enjoy the process

32 Cultivating Gratitude

Gratitude has the power to transform even the darkest of days into moments of light and grace. Today, cultivate an attitude of gratitude by focusing on the blessings in your life, no matter how small. Take stock of all that you have to be thankful for – your loved ones, your health, the beauty of nature. Allow gratitude to fill your heart and shift your perspective from lack to abundance.

Reflection: What are you grateful for in this moment? How does gratitude shift your perception of reality?

Action: Keep a gratitude journal and write down three things you're thankful for daily. Reflect on your entries and notice how gratitude enhances your sense of well-being.

YOUR NOTES:

Enjoy the process

Nourishing Self-Care

In times of grief, it's essential to prioritize self-care and nourish your body, mind, and soul. Today, indulge in self-care that replenishes your spirit and restores your energy. Whether taking a long bath, going for a nature walk, or practicing meditation, make time to honor your needs and nurture yourself with loving kindness.

Reflection: What self-care practices replenish you the most? How can you incorporate more self-care into your daily routine?

Action: Create a self-care plan for the week ahead, scheduling time each day for activities that nourish your body, mind, and soul. Commit to prioritizing your well-being and honoring your needs.

YOUR NOTES:

Enjoy the process

34 Seeking Support

Grief can feel overwhelming when faced alone, but it doesn't have to be. Today, reach out for support from friends, family, or professional counselors who can offer guidance and companionship on your journey. Allow yourself to be vulnerable and ask for help when you need it. Remember that you are not alone; some people care deeply about your well-being.

Reflection: Who can you turn to for support during times of grief? How can you strengthen your support network?

Action: Reach out to someone you trust and share your feelings openly and honestly. Allow yourself to receive their support and guidance with gratitude and humility.

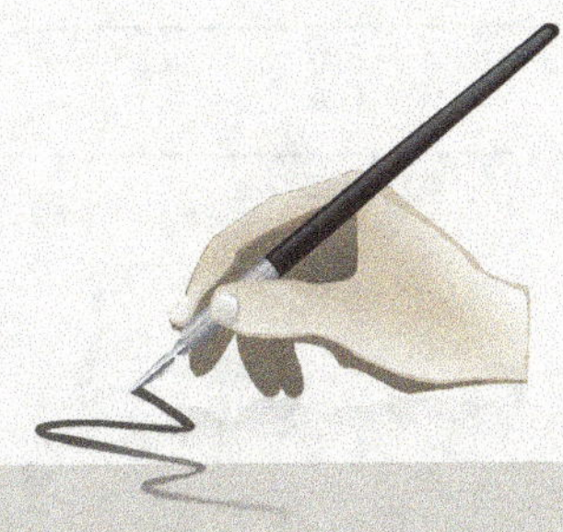

YOUR NOTES:

Enjoy the process

35 Embracing Hope

Hope is an expectation of a good that is yet to be. Hope is a belief that healing is possible. Hope is the beacon that guides us through the darkest of nights, reminding us that brighter days are ahead. It's also a belief that though today may not be the day you feel healed, there will be a future day that the feeling will happen. Today, embrace the hope that resides within you, even amid grief. Trust in the possibility of healing and transformation, knowing that every step you take brings you closer to grace. Embrace hope as your constant companion on the journey from darkness to light.

Reflection: What gives you hope in times of despair? How can you cultivate a sense of hopefulness in your life?

Action: Create a hope collage by gathering images, quotes, and symbols that inspire hope and optimism. Display it in a prominent place where you can see it daily, allowing it to serve as a reminder of the resilience of the human spirit. Listen to stories of people who have experienced a loss similar to yours in your quiet time.

YOUR NOTES:

Enjoy the process

36 Finding Strength in Vulnerability

Vulnerability is not a weakness but a courageous act of opening oneself to the depths of human experience. Today, embrace vulnerability as a source of strength on your journey from grief to grace. Allow yourself to be seen and heard, to share your struggles and triumphs with authenticity and courage. In vulnerability, you will find connection, empathy, and profound growth.

Reflection: How does vulnerability empower you on your journey of healing? What fears or reservations do you have about being vulnerable?

Action: Engage in an act of vulnerability today – share your feelings with a trusted friend, write a letter to yourself expressing your deepest emotions, or participate in a support group where you can openly discuss your experiences.

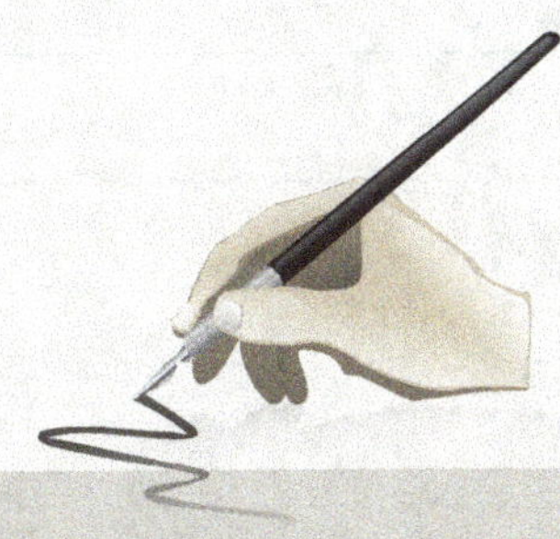

YOUR NOTES:

Enjoy the process

37 Cultivating Compassion

Compassion is the gentle hand that soothes the wounds of the heart and heals the pain of the soul. Today, cultivate compassion for yourself and others as you navigate the complexities of grief. Offer yourself grace in moments of struggle, acknowledging that you are doing the best you can with the resources you have. Extend compassion to others on their healing journey, recognizing that we are all interconnected in our shared humanity.

Reflection: How do you practice compassion in your life? How can you extend more compassion to yourself and others during grief?

Action: Practice a loving-kindness meditation, directing thoughts of compassion and goodwill towards yourself, loved ones, and all beings. Notice how cultivating compassion enhances your sense of connection and well-being.

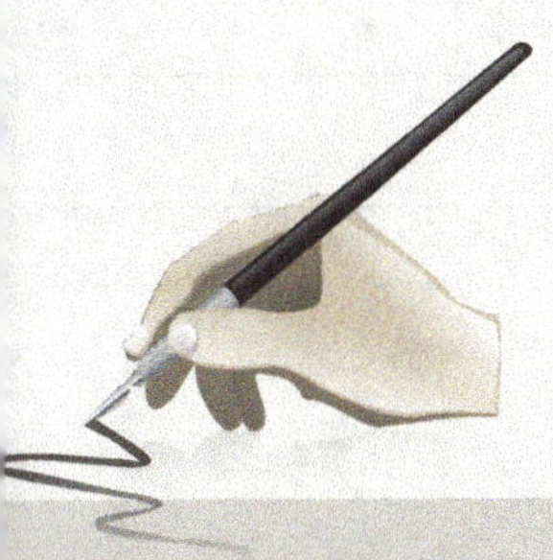

YOUR NOTES:

Enjoy the process

Restoring Balance

Grief can disrupt the delicate balance of life, leaving you feeling overwhelmed and out of sync. Today, focus on restoring balance by nurturing all aspects of your being – body, mind, and spirit. Pay attention to your physical needs for rest, nourishment, and movement. Engage in activities that bring you joy, peace, and fulfillment. Finding equilibrium amidst the chaos and knowing balance is essential for healing and well-being.

Reflection: How do you currently prioritize balance in your life? What areas could benefit from more attention and care?

Action: Create a balance wheel, dividing it into different areas of your life, such as work, relationships, health, and leisure. Assess your satisfaction with each location and identify areas you'd like to adjust to restore balance.

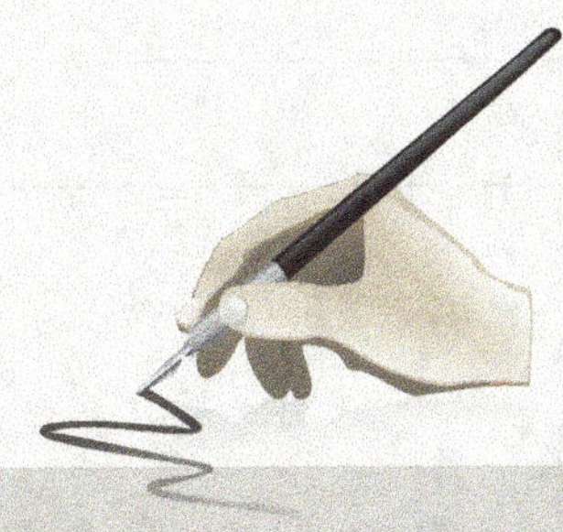

YOUR NOTES:

Enjoy the process

39 Honoring Memories

Memories are the threads that connect us to the past and anchor us in the present. Today, take time to honor the memories of loved ones who have passed away or experiences that have shaped your journey of grief. Celebrate the moments of joy, love, and connection shared with those no longer with you. Keep their memory alive, knowing they will always be a part of you.

Reflection: What memories hold special significance for you? How do they continue to influence your life today?

Action: Create a memory box or altar to honor your loved ones or significant life experiences. Fill it with photographs, souvenirs, and keepsakes that evoke cherished memories and moments of gratitude.

YOUR NOTES:

40 Embracing Impermanence

Impermanence is the natural rhythm of life, reminding us that everything is in a constant state of flux. Today, embrace the truth of impermanence as you navigate the ebb and flow of grief. Recognize that pain, like all things, is temporary and that joy and healing are also part of the cycle of life. Embrace each moment with presence and gratitude, knowing that every experience – both joyful and sorrowful – contributes to the richness of your journey.

Reflection: How do you relate to the concept of impermanence? How can embracing impermanence enhance your experience of grief and grace?

Action: Spend time in nature observing life's changing seasons and cycles. Reflect on the beauty and wisdom of impermanence, finding peace in the knowledge that change is an inherent part of the human experience.

YOUR NOTES:

Enjoy the process

41 Cultivating Resilience

Resilience is the ability to bounce back from adversity and emerge stronger and wiser than before. Today, cultivate resilience as you face the challenges of grief. Draw upon your inner strength and courage to navigate the ups and downs of the healing journey. Trust in your capacity to adapt, grow, and thrive in adversity. Remember that resilience is not about avoiding pain but embracing it with grace and grit.

Reflection: What experiences in your life have demonstrated your resilience? How can you cultivate resilience amid grief?

Action: Practice a resilience-building exercise such as journaling about past challenges you've overcome and identifying the strengths and coping strategies you utilized. Reflect on how these experiences have shaped your resilience and resilience.

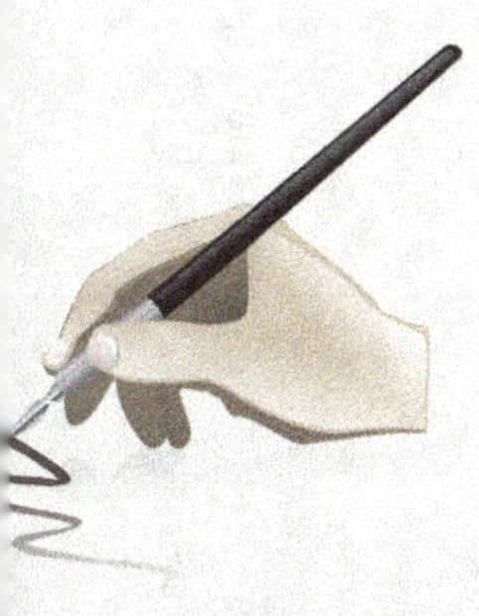

YOUR NOTES:

Enjoy the process

42 Finding Meaning amid Loss: Shifting Your Perspective

Beloved, while the "Why" might remain unanswered, finding meaning amid Loss is possible. Imagine a shattered vase, its pieces scattered on the ground. Though broken, the fragments still hold the beauty of the original design. Loss can feel like that – a shattering experience that leaves you feeling broken.

But consider this: the broken pieces can be repurposed and transformed into something new and beautiful. Your Loss has ignited a newfound appreciation for life, a deeper connection with loved ones, or a desire to help others going through similar experiences. Finding meaning doesn't erase the Loss but allows you to rebuild with the pieces you have left.

Reflection:
Think about the ways your life has changed since your Loss. Have you grown stronger, developed new skills, or discovered a deeper appreciation for certain things? Even in the darkness, can you find a glimmer of positive change?

Action:
Today, create a "gratitude jar." Write down things you're grateful for, big or small, on small pieces of paper. Focus on the positive ways your life has unfolded, even after the Loss. Place these notes in the jar and revisit them on challenging days for a reminder of the beauty that still exists.

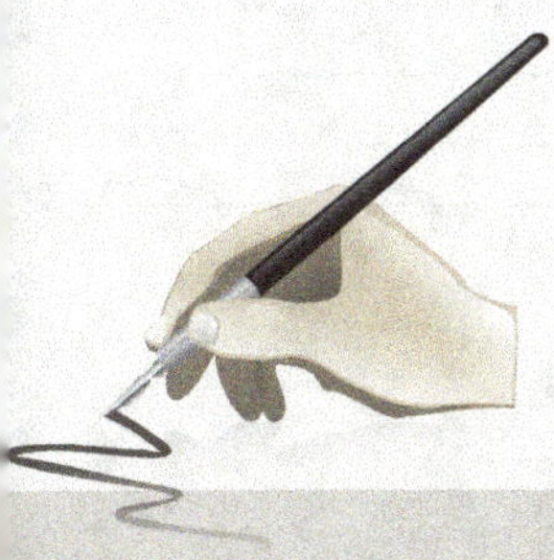

YOUR NOTES:

Enjoy the process

43 Connecting with Nature

Nature has a way of soothing the soul and providing solace in times of grief. Today, connect with the healing power of nature as you immerse yourself in its beauty and tranquility. Spend time outdoors, whether leisurely walking in the park, sitting by a babbling brook, or stargazing under the night sky. Allow nature's sights, sounds, and sensations to calm your mind, uplift your spirit, and remind you of the interconnectedness of all life.

Reflection: How does nature nurture your well-being? What are your favorite ways to connect with the natural world?

Action: Dedicate time today to engage in a nature-based activity that brings you joy and serenity. Connecting with nature enhances your sense of peace and presence in the moment.

YOUR NOTES:

44 Surrendering Control

Grief often brings a sense of powerlessness and uncertainty about the future. Today, practice surrendering control and trusting in the wisdom of life's unfolding. Release the need to micromanage every aspect of your journey and instead surrender to the flow of life. Trust that even amid uncertainty, a more excellent plan guides you toward healing, growth, and grace.

Reflection: Where do you struggle to surrender control in your life? What fears or beliefs contribute to this resistance?

Action: Engage in a surrender practice such as meditation, prayer, or deep breathing, letting go of the need to control outcomes and simply allowing yourself to be present with what is. Notice how surrendering control enhances your sense of peace and acceptance.

YOUR NOTES:

Enjoy the process

45 Setting Boundaries

In times of grief, setting boundaries that protect your emotional well-being and preserve your energy is essential. Today, reflect on the boundaries you must establish to honor your needs and values. Identify situations or relationships that drain your energy or trigger negative emotions, and consider how you can create healthier boundaries to protect yourself from harm.

Reflection: What boundaries do you need to set to prioritize your well-being? How can you communicate your boundaries assertively and respectfully?

Action: Take a proactive step towards setting boundaries by conversing with someone who consistently violates your boundaries. Communicate your needs and expectations, and assertively enforce your boundaries if necessary.

YOUR NOTES:

Enjoy the process

46 Seeking Meaning

Grief can catalyze profound introspection and growth, leading you to seek meaning in pain. Today, reflect on the more profound significance of your experiences with grief. Consider how they have shaped your values, beliefs, and priorities in life. Look for lessons and insights that can guide you on your journey of healing and transformation.

Reflection: What meaning can you find in your experiences of grief? How have they influenced the person you are today?

Action: Spend some time journaling about the lessons you've learned from your experiences with grief and how they have contributed to your personal growth and development.

YOUR NOTES:

Enjoy the process

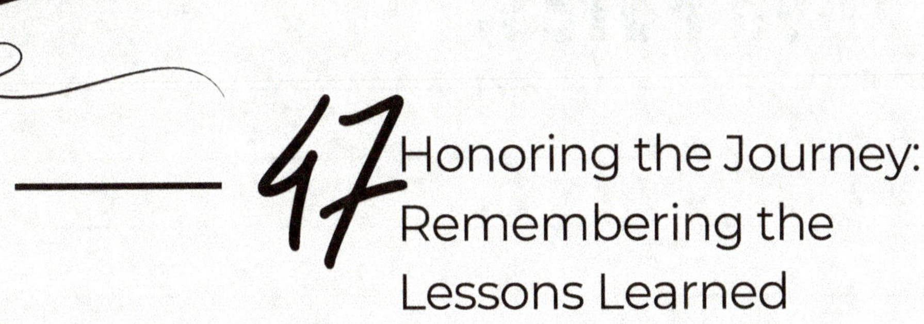

47 Honoring the Journey: Remembering the Lessons Learned

My dear friend, the "Why" might remain a mystery, but the lessons learned through your experience are invaluable. Imagine yourself on a long, winding road. The path may be filled with unexpected turns and obstacles, but it leads you to surprising destinations.

Loss, while painful, can be a catalyst for growth. You've learned the importance of cherishing loved ones, the power of resilience, and the beauty of living in the present moment. These lessons, though born from pain, can be a guiding light on your path forward.

Reflection:

Take some time to reflect on the lessons you've learned through your journey with grief. Has it taught you the importance of forgiveness, the strength of your spirit, or the power of human connection?

Action:

Today, write a letter to yourself, acknowledging the challenges you've faced and the strength you've shown. Express gratitude for the lessons learned and how you've grown through this experience. Remember, even in the face of unanswered questions, your journey holds valuable lessons that can guide you toward a brighter future.

YOUR NOTES:

Enjoy the process

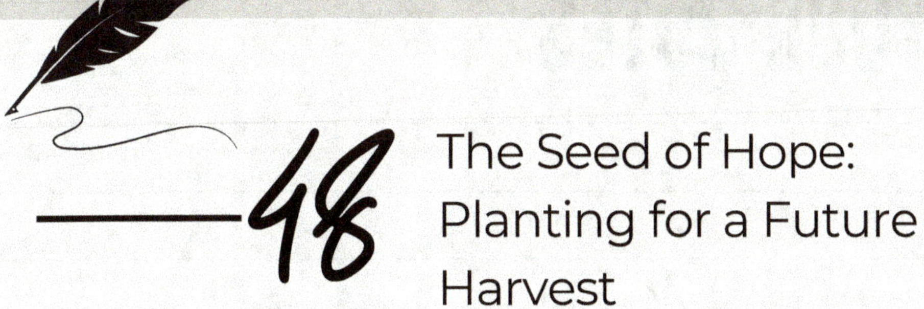

48 The Seed of Hope: Planting for a Future Harvest

My dear friend, grief can feel like a barren wasteland, a place where nothing can grow. But even in the most desolate landscape, a single seed holds the potential for abundant life. This seed represents hope, the promise of new beginnings even in the face of Loss.

Imagine yourself kneeling in the dirt, gently planting a seed. It's a small act, but it signifies your intention to move forward to cultivate a future filled with growth and purpose. You can't control the past, but you can choose how you nourish the present to create a flourishing future.

Reflection:

What are some small steps you can take to invest in your future? Is it enrolling in a class, pursuing a hobby, or setting achievable goals? Focus on planting those seeds of hope, no matter how small.

Action:

List three things you'd like to accomplish in the next month today. These could be personal or professional goals, big or small. Write them down with intention, visualizing yourself achieving each one. Remember, even the smallest seed, nurtured with care, can blossom into something beautiful.

YOUR NOTES:

Enjoy the process

49 Honoring the Past, Embracing the Present: Stepping into the Now

My dear friend, moving on doesn't mean forgetting the past or erasing your memories. It's about acknowledging their importance while focusing your energy on the present moment. Imagine yourself standing at a crossroads, one path leading back to the past, the other towards an unknown future.

The past holds invaluable lessons and cherished memories. But to truly move forward, you must focus on the present moment. This is where you can take action, make choices, and cultivate a fulfilling life.

Reflection:

Take a few deep breaths and focus on the present moment. Notice the sights, sounds, and sensations around you. Are you dwelling on the past or worrying about the future? Gently bring your attention back to the present, where you have the power to create a life filled with purpose.

Action:

Today, practice a simple mindfulness exercise. Find a comfortable position and focus on your breath. As thoughts arise, acknowledge them without judgment and gently return your attention to the present moment. Remember, living in the present allows you to move forward gracefully and intentionally.

YOUR NOTES:

Enjoy the process

50 Small Steps, Big Impact: Embracing the Power of Productivity

My dear friend, navigating grief can feel overwhelming, making it challenging to find the motivation to be productive. However, taking small steps can be incredibly empowering. Imagine climbing a mountain, one step at a time. No matter how small, each step brings you closer to the summit.

Start with achievable tasks. It could be making your bed, completing a small chore, or spending focused time on a project. Accomplishing these tasks, however minor, boosts your mood and builds a sense of accomplishment. It allows you to reclaim a sense of control over your life.

Reflection:

Consider your current schedule and identify areas where you can incorporate small acts of productivity. Is it starting your day with a simple morning routine, setting aside dedicated work time, or completing a task on your to-do list?

Action:

Today, choose one small task that has been weighing on your mind. Set a timer for 15 minutes and focus solely on completing that task. Celebrate your accomplishments, no matter how minor, and acknowledge the power of small steps in moving forward.

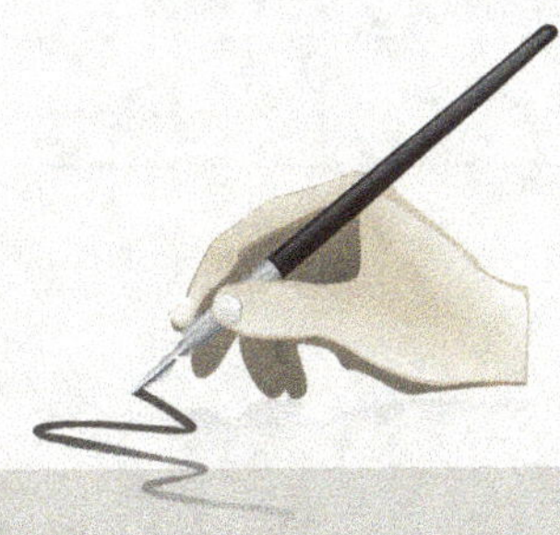

YOUR NOTES:

Enjoy the process

51 Finding Joy in the Journey: Embracing Imperfection

My dear friend, moving on and being productive is not about achieving perfection. Imagine yourself painting a beautiful landscape, not a flawless one. There will be moments of darkness, splashes of unexpected colors, and even strokes that seem out of place.

Grief is a natural part of the landscape of your life. Embrace the imperfections, the moments of sadness alongside the moments of joy. It's in navigating these emotions that you discover your strength and resilience.

Reflection:

Take a moment to reflect on your journey with grief. Have there been moments of productivity alongside moments of sorrow? Acknowledge the beauty and complexity of your emotions, and celebrate the small victories along the way.

Action:

Today, create a visual representation of your journey with grief. It could be a painting, a drawing, or even a collage. Allow yourself to express your emotions freely, without judgment. Remember, your journey is unique, filled with darkness and light, and that's perfectly okay.

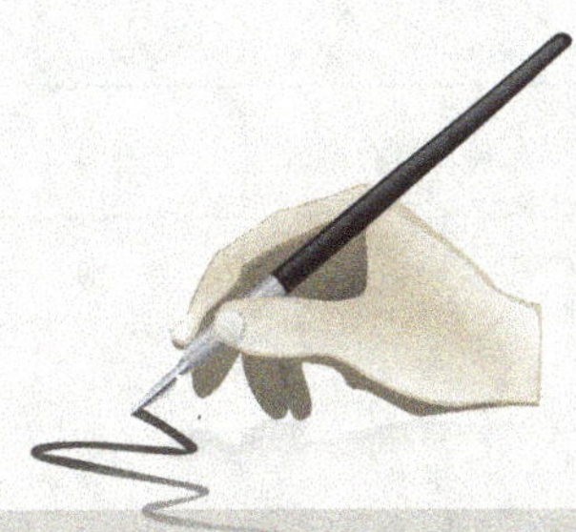

YOUR NOTES:

Enjoy the process

52 Returning to Work: Carrying Strength and Hope

My dear friend, as the fog of grief begins to lift, you might face a return to the workplace. This can be a daunting prospect, filled with a mix of emotions. Perhaps you're worried about your ability to focus, concerned about emotional triggers, or simply unsure how to navigate a new normal.

Imagine yourself standing at the doorway of your workplace. You may feel hesitant, even a little afraid. But remember, you are not alone. You carry the strength you've cultivated through your journey with grief and the hope for a brighter future.

Reflection:

Take a few deep breaths and acknowledge your emotions. Is there nervousness, excitement, or a combination of both? It's perfectly okay to feel a range of emotions as you return to work. Allow yourself to experience them without judgment.

Action:

Today, practice some self-compassion. Write down a positive affirmation for yourself, such as "I am strong," "I am capable," or "I will get through this." Place this affirmation somewhere you'll see it often, like your desk or phone background, as a reminder of your inner strength.

YOUR NOTES:

Enjoy the process

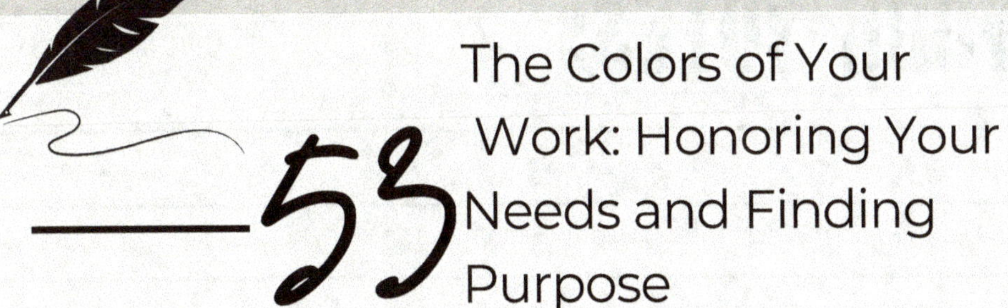

The Colors of Your Work: Honoring Your Needs and Finding Purpose

Darling, returning to work can be an opportunity to rediscover a sense of purpose and routine. Imagine yourself as an artist, picking up your paintbrush for the first time since your Loss. The canvas may feel blank, the colors unfamiliar, but the creativity and resilience to paint a new masterpiece lie within you.

This means returning to something other than the exact work you knew before. Your priorities have shifted. Consider ways to honor your needs in the workplace. Communicate openly with your employer about any adjustments you might require, whether a flexible schedule, a reduced workload, or access to an employee assistance program.

Reflection:

Think about what brought you satisfaction in your work before your Loss. Was it the sense of accomplishment, the social interaction, or the intellectual challenge? Can you find ways to incorporate these elements into your work now?

Action:

Today, brainstorm ways to add purpose back into your work. It could be taking on a new project, volunteering your skills within the company, or simply focusing on one task at a time with renewed dedication. Remember, even small changes can make a big difference in your work experience.

YOUR NOTES:

Enjoy the process

54 Sharing Your Story: Finding Connection and Support at Work

My dear friend, navigating grief in the workplace can feel isolating. But you don't have to go through this alone. Imagine yourself standing in a room filled with colleagues. Some may know about your Loss; others may not. Sharing your story, even in a small way, can be a powerful tool for finding connection and support.

It doesn't have to be a grand announcement. It could be a simple conversation with a trusted co-worker or mentioning the reason behind an adjusted schedule. Sharing your experience opens the door for others to offer empathy and understanding. You might be surprised by the outpouring of support from your work community.

Reflection:

Think about who feels safe and supportive in your workplace. Is there someone you trust enough to confide in about your grief journey? Perhaps it's a colleague who has also experienced Loss or simply someone who is a good listener.

Action:

Today, consider reaching out to a supportive colleague. You can start by acknowledging the awkwardness of returning to work after a loss or share a brief update about your situation. Remember, even small acts of connection can make a big difference in feeling supported at work.

YOUR NOTES:

Enjoy the process

55 Planting Seeds for the Future: Investing in Growth

You've come a long way on this 60-day journey. Not only have you navigated the challenges of loss, you've also planted seeds for a secure financial future. Now is the time to think about growth.

Reflection:
Consider your long-term financial goals. Do you dream of owning a home? Are you saving for retirement? The clearer your goals, the better you can invest your resources today.

Action:
Today, research different investment options. Talk to a financial advisor if needed. Even a small investment can grow significantly over time. Remember, it's never too late to start planting seeds for a brighter financial future.

YOUR NOTES:

Enjoy the process

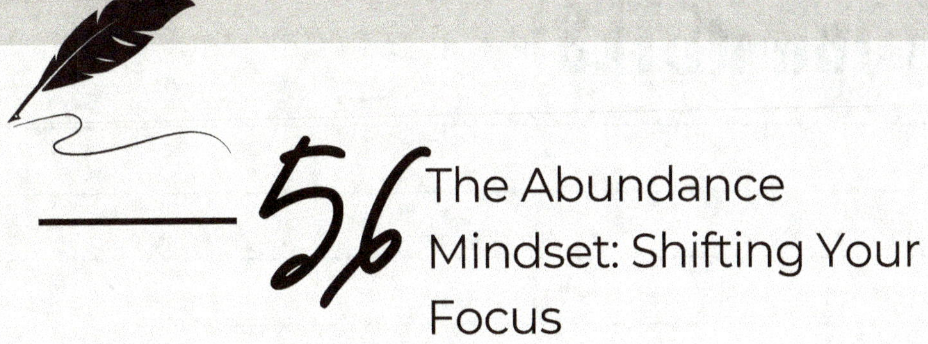

56 The Abundance Mindset: Shifting Your Focus

Grief can make you feel like you're constantly lacking. However, focusing solely on scarcity can trap you in a cycle of fear and limitation. Instead, cultivate an abundance mindset, believing there are enough resources to meet your needs.

Reflection:
Think about times in your life when you weren't sure how you'd make ends meet, but somehow things worked out. These experiences can be proof of the abundance that surrounds you, even in challenging times.

Action:
Today, challenge yourself to find examples of abundance in your life, not just financial. Maybe you have a supportive network of friends, good health, or access to public libraries and parks. Recognizing abundance attracts more abundance.

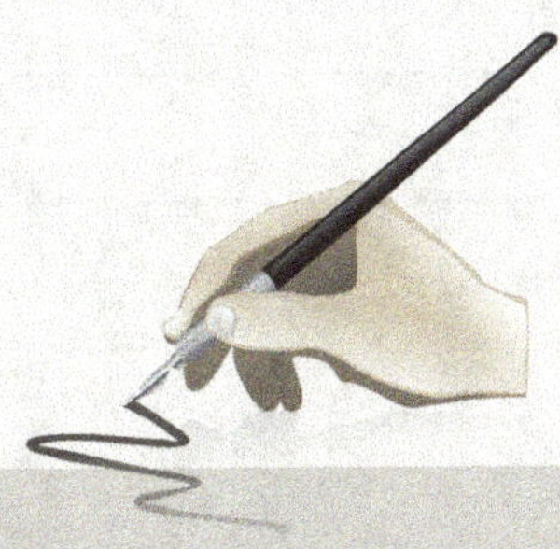

YOUR NOTES:

Enjoy the process

57 Budgeting During Difficult Times

Remember that stack of financial statements we collected? Today, let's use them to create a budget. A budget might sound restrictive, but it's actually a tool for empowerment. It allows you to take control of your finances and prioritize your spending.

Reflection:

Think about your essential expenses – housing, food, utilities. Then consider other needs and wants. Be honest with yourself about where your money goes.

Action:

There are many budgeting apps and tools available online. Choose one that works for you, or simply use a pen and paper. List your income sources and then categorize your expenses. Be realistic and don't be afraid to adjust as needed.

58 Finding Your Financial Footing After Loss

Loss can turn your world upside down, and that includes your finances. Maybe you're dealing with unexpected bills, a change in income, or simply the emotional toll that makes focusing on money tough. Whatever your situation, this devotional is here to help you find your financial footing again.

Reflection:

Take a few minutes to breathe and acknowledge where you're at. Do you have a general idea of your income and expenses? Are there any immediate financial concerns you need to address? Writing it all down can help you see things more clearly.

Action:

Today, schedule some time to gather your financial statements – bank accounts, credit card bills, recent pay stubs. Having a clear picture of your financial situation is the first step to moving forward.

YOUR NOTES:

Enjoy the process

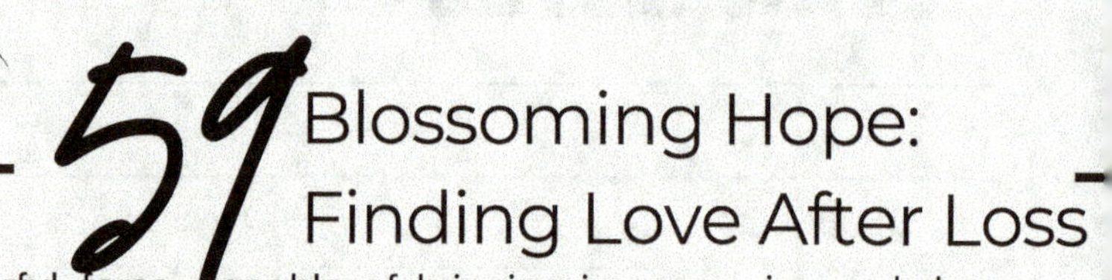

59 Blossoming Hope: Finding Love After Loss

Love is a powerful force, capable of bringing immense joy and deep connection. After experiencing Loss, the thought of opening your heart again feels daunting. It's natural to wonder if you can love again or if anyone can understand the depth of your grief.

Imagine yourself standing in a garden where once vibrant flowers had wilted. Though some may be gone, the soil still holds the potential for new life. Love, like the seeds within that soil, never truly dies. You can choose to nurture it again, allowing it to bloom anew.

Reflection:

Take a moment to reflect on your emotions. Are you open to the possibility of finding love again? Perhaps you fear being hurt or feel disloyal to the one you lost. Acknowledge these emotions without judgment. Grief doesn't erase your capacity for love; it simply transfoms it.

Action:

Today, practice self-compassion. Write a letter acknowledging your pain and affirming your worthiness of love. Allow yourself to grieve, but also open your heart to the possibility of a future filled with new connections.

Remember, love doesn't replace what you lost; it enriches your life differently. When the time feels right, consider exploring ways to meet new people through friends, social groups, or online platforms. Focus on building genuine connections, and trust that love will find you when your heart is ready to receive it.

YOUR NOTES:

Enjoy the process

60 Nurturing the Seeds of Recovery

My dear friend, today marks a new chapter in your journey. You are now at the end of this road. But the journey doesn't end here. Growth is a continuous process and never really stops. You only get better than you were before and onwards.

Why 60 Days? This timeframe allowed for consistent action and the formation of new habits. It's long enough to see progress but short enough to feel manageable.

Reflection: Dedicate time for self-reflection. What are your emotional needs? What brings you a sense of accomplishment? Write down your goals, both personal and professional.

Support System: Identify your support network – friends, family, therapists, or support groups. Reach out to them and build a schedule for regular connections.

Self-Care: Prioritize activities that nourish your mind, body, and spirit. This could be meditation, leisure time in nature, or a creative hobby.

Planning for Productivity:

Small Steps: Break down significant goals into achievable daily tasks. Celebrate even minor victories as they pave the way for more substantial accomplishments.

Prioritization: Identify the most critical tasks on your plate and dedicate focused time to them. Learn to say "no" to tasks that drain your energy without adding value.

Reward System: Celebrate your progress with meaningful rewards. A relaxing evening with friends, a new book, or a nature hike can serve as motivational incentives.

Remember, this is your plan. It's flexible and can be adjusted as your needs evolve. Feel free to experiment and find what works best for you.

Action:

Today, dedicate some time to planning your journey. Start by identifying your top 3 goals for recovery and productivity. Remember, you are not alone. With each step, you cultivate resilience, reclaim your purpose, and enter a brighter future. Get volume 2 of "A pen that rewrites grief" to continue your journey of self-discovery.

YOUR NOTES:

Enjoy the process

SMART GOALS MAPPING

Concrete goals are your milestones. Let's set
goals that are SMART:

S	Specific: Clear and concise.

M	Measurable: Quantifiable to track progress.

A	Achievable: Attainable to remain motivating.

R	Relevant: Aligned with your larger wellness vision.

T	Time-bound: Encased within a timeframe.

*Sketch your goals with kindness, remembering that they are
fluid and can adapt to your journey's needs.*

SELF-CARE CHECKLIST

*Self-care isn't an act but a loving commitment to oneself.
How did you cherish yourself this week?*

- [ ] Take a long bath
- [ ] Read for pleasure
- [ ] Go for a long walk
- [ ] Practice mindful meditation

- [ ] Engage in a hobby
- [ ] Listen to your favorite music
- [ ] Spend time with a loved one
- [ ] Watch a light-hearted movie

- [ ] Journal your thoughts
- [ ] Try gentle yoga
- [ ] Cook a nourishing meal
- [ ] Visit a museum or gallery
- [ ] Gardening
- [ ] Paint or draw

- [ ] Pamper yourself
- [ ] Take a short nap
- [ ] Go for a swim
- [ ] Practice gratitude
- [ ] Attend a workshop or class
- [ ] Explore a new place

A PEN THAT REWRITES GRIEF

To do's

01. Set Weekly Intentions

Reflect on a theme or feeling you'd like to
guide your week and jot it down.

02. SMART Goals Mapping

Outline some tangible goals for your week.

03. Daily Check-In

Every evening, take a moment to reflect on your day,
noting down your activities, joys, and challenges.

04. Self-Care & Relaxation

Keep track of your dedicated self-care moments
through the week.

05. Weekly Reflections

At the end of the week, spend time reviewing,
celebrating wins, and recognizing lessons.

Daily Reflection

3 things I'm grateful for.

Today, Good that Happened to Me an

Today,

this not so good thing happened to me and this is how I handled it:

Today, this thing made me happy:

Today, I discovered this about myself:

WEEKLY REFLECTIONS

WINS OF THE WEEK

Celebrate your achievements, however small they might be:

CHALLENGES ENCOUNTERED

Acknowledge any struggles or bottlenecks you faced:

LESSONS LEARNED

Identify learnings that can be carried forward:

NEXT WEEK'S PRELIMINARY THOUGHTS

Write down any early ideas or focus points for the upcoming week:

Conclusion: Embracing the Journey

Hello friend, we've walked together these past Sixty days, exploring the pathways of grief, healing, and growth. You've faced challenges, navigated uncertainties, and planted the seeds for a brighter future. Remember, this journey is not a linear path. There will be days filled with sunshine and days shrouded in rain. But even in the storm, you carry the strength and resilience you've cultivated.

As you move forward, carry these reminders close to your heart:

Your grief is valid. Allow yourself to feel the full range of emotions without judgment.

You are not alone. Lean on your support system and seek professional help if needed.

Healing takes time. Be patient with yourself and celebrate even the most minor victories.

Embrace self-care. Nourish your mind, body, and spirit with activities that bring you peace.

Find meaning in your Loss. Honor the one you love by living your life to the fullest. Don't forget to grab Volume 2 and leave a Review. If you need to join a community, Join us Echoes Of Life @ www.echoesoflfe.org where you can share with other people who have/ are navigating grief.

Thank you
FOR READING

CONGRATULATIONS ON COMPLETING THIS JOURNEY OF NAVIGATING GRIEF

Join our Podcast on all platform where real people share their life journey navigating from

GRIEF 2 GRACE

WWW.GRIEF2GRACE.COM
f GRIEF2GRACE

RUTH HEPHZIBAH